ROWING IN
BRITAIN

Julie Summers

SHIRE PUBLICATIONS

Published in Great Britain in 2012 by Shire Publications
Ltd, Midland House, West Way, Botley, Oxford OX2 0PH,
United Kingdom.

44-02 23rd Street, Suite 219, Long Island City, NY 11101,
USA.

E-mail: shire@shirebooks.co.uk   www.shirebooks.co.uk

A CIP catalogue record for this book is available from the
British Library.

Shire Library no. 717.   ISBN-13: 978 0 74781 211 1

Julie Summers has asserted her right under the Copyright,
Designs and Patents Act, 1988, to be identified as the
author of this book.

Designed by Tony Truscott Designs, Sussex, UK
and typeset in Perpetua and Gill Sans.

Printed in China through Worldprint Ltd.

12 13 14 15 16   10 9 8 7 6 5 4 3 2 1

COVER IMAGE

Rowing, colour lithograph by Maurice and Jacques Goddet,
published in *Les Joies du Sport*, Paris 1932.

TITLE PAGE IMAGE

The Oxford and Cambridge Boat Race, *c.* 1871, published
in London and Hamburg by S. Lipschitz.

CONTENTS PAGE IMAGE

University eight training on the Isis, *c.* 1866, published by
William Mackenzie, London, Edinburgh and Glasgow.

ACKNOWLEDGEMENTS

Julie Summers thanks Martin Humphreys and Lady
Hanmer for permission to use a private letter as
inspiration for 'One Foot'. She would like to extend warm
thanks to the following for their help and support: Kneale
Barber, Di Binley, Isabel Boanas-Evans, Eloise Chapman,
Lisa Cochrane, Christopher Dodd, Annabel Eyres, Adam
Freeman-Pask, Lindsay Guest, Janie Hampton, Martin
Humphreys, Paul Mainds, Peter McConnell, Colin
Middlemiss, Sara Nanayakkara, Richard Owen, Michal V.
Palamarczuk, Nick Putnam, Nick Randall, John Shore,
Simon Steele, Sheila Stephens, Andy Thomson, Robert
Treharne Jones, Paul Vicars, Julia Walworth, Sarah Wearne,
Frances Wilmoth and Denise Gabrielle Yebes Yap-Lintag.

IMAGE ACKNOWLEDGEMENTS

Abingdon School, page 15 (bottom); Bigblade
Photography, page 7; Company of Watermen and
Lightermen, page 10; Annabel Eyres, page 35; Adam
Freeman-Pask, page 27 (bottom); Furnivall Sculling Club,
page 22; Janie Hampton, page 17 (bottom) and 52 (top);
Henley Royal Regatta © Oepkes.com, pages 5, 6; John
Hale, page 26 (bottom); by permission of the Master and
Fellows of Jesus College, Cambridge, photographer Simon
Tottman, page 15 (top); Leander Club, pages 19, 20; The
Warden and Trustees of Merton College, Oxford, pages
31, 37; PA History, page 23 (top); River and Rowing
Museum, Henley, pages 1, 3, 9, 11 (all images), 14, 16, 18
(bottom), 23 (bottom), 24, 27 (top), 28, 30 (bottom),
32–3, 34 (bottom), 36 (top), 38 (top), 38 (bottom), 40,
42 (top), 42 (bottom), 43, 44, 45, 46, 47, 50, 51; Royal
Chester Rowing Club, pages 12, 21; John Shore, pages 39,
52 (bottom), 54; Peter Spurrier, pages 25 (bottom), 37
(bottom), 48, 49, 53 (top), 53 (bottom); The Stapleton
Collection / The Bridgeman Art Library, cover image;
Sandy Steele, page 13; Julie Summers, pages 18 (top), 26
(top), 34 (top); The Master and Fellows of University
College, Oxford, page 30 (top).

Shire Publications is supporting the Woodland Trust, the UK's leading woodland conservation charity, by funding the dedication of trees.

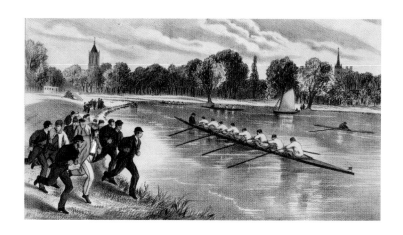

CONTENTS

ONE FOOT

SUNDAY 8 July 2007 and the market town of Henley-on-Thames is enjoying a warm afternoon. On the Berkshire bank of the river the scene is one of colour, pageantry and tradition: blue-and-white striped boat tents marshalled neatly between the pink-and-cream Leander Club hard up against Henley Bridge, and the white marquees housing the grandstands and Stewards' Enclosure on the downstream side. It is finals day of the regatta, the day when lives are changed for ever by the outcome of an individual race. At 3:50pm two crews of nine young men line up at the start, next to the lozenge-shaped island in the middle of the river crowned by an elegant temple designed by the eighteenth-century English architect, James Wyatt. The umpire is standing in a handsome launch, arms raised, holding a red flag vertically above his head waiting for the two coxes to indicate that their crews are all set. *Are you ready?* He sweeps the flag down sharply. *Go!* Sixteen blades dip into the water. They are off.

There is expectation and excitement all along the river bank – not least in the Stewards' Enclosure where nervous parents fidget, check their watches, exchange anxious glances and wonder why the commentator has not mentioned the race yet. But patience. Then the deadpan announcement over the loudspeaker: *The final of the Princess Elizabeth Challenge Cup is in progress between Brentwood College School on the Berkshire station and Shrewsbury School on the Bucks station. Brentwood College School are the Canadian National School Champions.* No mention of Shrewsbury's pedigree.

Upwards of 100,000 people attend Henley Royal Regatta each July. It is an event caught in a bubble of history with echoes of a bygone era everywhere: fine hats, striped blazers, picnics in the car park come rain or shine, decorated launches bobbing on the white booms that line the course, Pimms jugs clinking with ice, champagne and oysters, a brass band playing military tunes, and all the while a titanic battle is being fought on the water. Brentwood had dispatched the favourites, Eton, in the semi-finals the day before and Shrewsbury had beaten Radley in a slower time.

At the end of the island, both crews rating 42, Brentwood College School lead Shrewsbury School by half a length. Forty strokes in from the start and the Canadians already have a half-length lead. Six minutes to go. The grandstand is full of Shrewsbury supporters. There is barely a free seat, the atmosphere tense. Elsewhere people are milling around the bars and chatting. Henley is, after all, a great social event. It marks the end of the summer season, after Ascot, and coincides with finals day at Wimbledon.

At The Barrier, Brentwood College School maintained their lead of half a length over Shrewsbury School. Time to The Barrier, 1 minute 58 seconds. A buzz. One second faster than yesterday. The Barrier is one of two points where intermediate times are taken, times that later will be scrutinised, compared,

The umpire starts a race at Henley Royal Regatta, which he will follow in the launch. In earlier times races were started by pistol or cannon and at the first Henley regatta the umpire followed on horseback.

5

Spectators sitting on stools close to the finish line at Henley Royal Regatta. The course is longer than the standard 2-km regatta course by 112 metres and this sometimes causes problems for crews unused to rowing Henley's 1 mile and 550 yards.

delighted at or despaired over. The spectators downstream can see the action first. Crowding along the river bank they get close-up views of the two crews battling it out in the early stages of the race.

The next timing point is Fawley. Now there is a change: *At Fawley, Brentwood College School's lead over Shrewsbury School has been reduced to a quarter of a length.* The grandstand is in spasm; spectators begin to move towards the river bank sensing a spectacle. Downstream the shouting has increased and the excitement is palpable. Can the home crew crack the Canadians? *At The Three-Quarter Mile Signal Brentwood School led Shrewsbury School by 2 feet.* The grandstand is on its feet, a roar moving up the bank like a giant wave. Half the race gone. *At the Mile Signal, Shrewsbury School had taken the lead.* Wild elation but fear too. The Canadians were not about to give up and Shrewsbury supporters knew that. 'We could see them now and it looked like hell', wrote housemaster Martin Humphreys to crew member Tom Hanmer's parents. 'Shrewsbury on the far side pounding away, looking a bit scrappy and tired, to be honest. Brentwood on the near side and neat and long. When they came past us Shrewsbury had a quarter of a length lead, but I could see the Canadians were eating into it with every stroke. This was grim.' The two boats cross the line neck and neck. Then there is silence. The commentary ceases and the Finish Judge has to make his call. The wait seems interminable; time stands still. Then: *The result of the Final of the Princess Elizabeth Challenge Cup was that Shr ...* No need for the rest: the name of the winning crew is always announced first. The grandstand explodes in ecstasy ... *the verdict, one foot.* More cheering. The narrowest, the shortest, the tiniest of winning margins imaginable, less than a sixtieth of the length of the boat.

For Brentwood College School a bitter blow. To be a member of a losing crew, however epic the race, there are no prizes. For the boys of the winning crew and their parents, unsurpassed joy, a matter of lifetime pride and for one man in particular this is a sweet victory. Eighty-three-year-old Michael Lapage watched his grandson, Patrick, help to win this great battle. Nearly seventy years earlier, on the same stretch of river, Michael had won silver for Great Britain in the 1948 Olympic Games. The legacy of a Henley win is a long one. It unites generations and brings tears to the eyes of the strongest of men.

Shrewsbury on the near side pushing Brentwood on the far side right to the line in the 2007 final of the Princess Elizabeth Challenge Cup.

THE RISE OF
COMPETITIVE
ROWING

'VENETIANS may claim to have originated the regatta, but the British were the pioneers of moving across water while sitting down and facing backwards', wrote journalist and rowing historian, Christopher Dodd, in his book *The Story of World Rowing* published in 1992. Rowing is indeed one of the only sports that involve the athlete going backwards at speed. Technically it can be described as the art of propelling a boat by the reaction forces on the oar blades as they are pushed against the water. To those who practice the sport at all levels it is the art of balancing power and technique in order to make the boat 'sing' – that is, to move smoothly with maximum efficiency. It is a great deal more difficult than it looks. There are many types

Roman trireme, from a mosaic at Carthage.

of rowing and almost as many types of races. For the purpose of this brief history we will concentrate on sweep-oar rowing and sculling, both of which are competed for at Olympic level.

The history of rowing can be traced back as far as the ancient Greeks, who propelled massive, three-tiered boats called triremes, and through the Vikings and Venetians. But modern rowing, as recognised by members of the public who tune in to the annual Oxford and Cambridge Boat Race, was developed in England in the eighteenth century. It was consolidated and codified in the nineteenth (predominantly by Oxbridge students who had been at Eton, Westminster or one of the other public schools that were early adopters of the sport), and spread to metropolitan clubs along all the major rivers in Britain. By the early years of the twentieth century rowing had been taken up as a sport in countries throughout the world. The majority of rowing events take place with little interest shown by the outside world, but twice a year in Britain and once every four years on the world stage, rowing becomes visible.

For centuries the rivers of Britain's cities were used for trade, transport and engineering, long before pleasure became a fashionable concept in Victorian Britain. Royalty used the Thames as the most efficient way of travelling between the Royal Palaces of Windsor, Westminster, Hampton Court, Greenwich and the Tower of London. The Royal Barge was powered

Henley after a race, 1893, based on an illustration by Dickenson and Foster.

by eight oarsmen in full livery: a skirted scarlet tunic with a silver gilt Royal Cypher (plastrum) on the front and back of the jacket, breeches, navy or black cap, scarlet stockings, white shirt and black buckled shoes. Bargemaster is one of the most ancient appointments in the Royal Household and although the role has been purely ceremonial since the mid-nineteenth century, the Sovereign still maintains twenty-four Royal Watermen under The Queen's Bargemaster. These oarsmen are selected from the ranks of the Thames Watermen, who in the twenty-first century man tugs, lighters and launches. In previous centuries the Watermen's and Lightermen's company regulated employment in London and a long apprenticeship was required before it was possible to work on the tidal section of the river. They were also responsible for ferrying people across the river in an era of few bridges over the Thames. One grateful passenger was Thomas Doggett, an Irish actor and comedian who relied on the Watermen of the Thames to ferry him to his workplaces in the City of London and offered a rowing wager 'to the fastest six young Watermen in their first year of freedom'. This race was first rowed on 1 August 1715 from The Swan pub at London Bridge to The Swan pub at Chelsea. Doggett organised and financed the race for six years until his death in 1721 and in his will left specific instructions for it to continue. The race has been organised annually since 1722 over the same course, though neither pub exists. The winning oarsman was, and is still, awarded the Doggett's

The Doggett's winners, in full livery, rowing the Lord Mayor, Alderman David Wootton, to the start of his Lord Mayor's Show on 12 November 2011.

coat, cap, breeches and silver badge, based on the original eighteenth-century costumes.

The river was also used by private individuals. Noblemen had their own craft with liveried oarsmen and there was often competition between these

Left: Dick Phelps, winner of the Doggett's Coat and Badge, 1923, in full regalia.

Above: Doggett's badge won by Charles 'Wag' Harding in 1888. The badge depicts the white horse of Hanover with 'Liberty' for the motto; Doggett wished to commemorate the accession of George I, to whom, as a Whig, he was devoted.

Members of the Amalgamated Society of Watermen and Lightermen, 1911–12.

boats either for pride, or more often than not, for wagers. The oarsman and rowing coach, Gilbert Bourne (1861–1933), summed up the equivalence of the various eighteenth-century boats owned and run by aristocrats in his *Textbook of Oarsmanship*:

> The eight-oared boat was the aquatic equivalent of the coach and six; costly to maintain, splendid in its equipment, and appropriate only to great persons … a six-oar would have the rank of a coach and four, a four-oar of a carriage and pair, and lesser craft would represent the one-horsed carriages of humbler folk.

In modern rowing the two main types of boats are classed according to whether the oarsman rows with one oar or two. In sweep-oar rowing, or 'sweep' as it is often known, each rower has one oar which is held in both hands. Unlike other boats which refer to the left and right as port or starboard, rowing boats have a stroke side and a bow side. The stroke side is on the oarsman's right and the bow side is on his or her left. Sweep is rowed in combinations of two rowers, so there are pairs, fours and eights. An eight actually comprises nine people as the boat is steered by a coxswain or, in its regularly shortened form, cox. The cox faces the rowers and steers the boat by pulling on wires which are attached to the rudder, while calling

According to legend, eight kings of Britain rowed King Edgar down the River Dee in AD 973.

instructions to the crew. Fours may be either coxed or coxless. A pair is usually, but not exclusively, coxless. A coxless four is steered by any member of the crew who has the rudder cable attached to the toe of one of their shoes (fixed to a footplate in the boat) which can be pivoted right or left to change direction. Often the oarsman in the bow seat steers as he or she has the best view over the shoulder. One bowman likened steering to 'swapping both sides of your brain over and imagining you are reversing around the Périphérique in Paris'. A successful steersman, like a good cox, has to know the river well and be confident in the racing line, while negotiating other crews. It can be a fine balancing act and misjudgement can end in a lost race, a clash with another boat, or worse.

Sculling boats have two oars per person and are composed of pairs, with the exception of the single scull for one person, which is best described as a cigar-shaped boat, with a balance problem. Doubles, quadruple sculls and (for junior scullers only) octuple sculls have four, eight or sixteen blades respectively.

In the North of England, life on the Tyne was as busy as in London and as industrialisation took hold, Newcastle thrived. Shipbuilding and heavy engineering were the mainstays of industry between the city and the sea. The port had developed in the sixteenth century but it was in the middle of the nineteenth that the Newcastle Corporation made the river more navigable. As one of the world's largest shipbuilding and ship-repair centres it fostered innovation and produced some of the most impressive oarsmen and boat-builders whose technical developments influenced rowing throughout Britain. Tyneside oarsmen are credited with at least two of the key developments in racing boat technology. As Dodd writes:

> Their technical developments profoundly affected events such as the world professional sculling championship, the Oxford and Cambridge Boat Race, and regattas such as Chester, Durham and Henley. In the mid-nineteenth century rowing was followed widely in England, and Tyneside names like Clasper, Taylor, Swaddle and Winship were etched on the history of racing boat design.

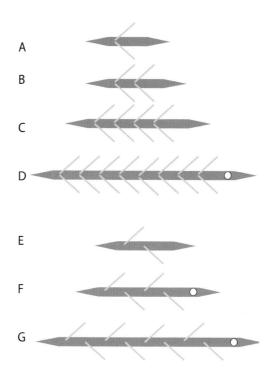

Sweep-oar and sculling boats.
A: Single scull
B: Double scull
C: Quadruple scull
D: Octuple
E: Pair
F: Coxed four
G: Eight

Harry Clasper fitted outriggers to a four in 1845 and the following year both Oxford and Cambridge used them in the Boat Race. The outrigger is a triangular metal frame that holds the rowlock, into which the oar is slotted, away from the boat, to optimise leverage. The beauty of the triangular outrigger was that it allowed for a narrower boat, which was lighter and drew less in the water.

Matthew Taylor was a ship's carpenter from Newcastle, a professional sculler and a contemporary of Clasper. He was instrumental in changing the shape and design of rowing boats. In 1854 he built a smooth-bottomed boat for Royal Chester Rowing Club, bringing the keel inboard and reducing the weight considerably. In 1855 the club used this boat at Henley Royal Regatta and won the Stewards' Challenge Cup. Taylor then received orders from both Chester and Oxford University Boat Club for eights. Taylor's boats were lighter than other boats and they offered less friction in the water since the maximum width of the boat was placed well forward. Oxford won the Boat Race in a Taylor keel-less boat in 1857.

The two other developments were the introduction of the swivel rowlock and the sliding seat. It was the latter that marked the difference between traditional and modern rowing and was introduced by the Americans in 1872. 'Broadly speaking, slides meant that the length of stroke was increased and the power of the legs could be brought into play.' It also had the effect, Christopher Dodd explains, of changing the shape of the ideal rower from a stocky man with a powerful back and torso, to a taller athlete with longer limbs since the power was now driven by the legs.

Sliding of a sort had been practised in Britain by professional rowers, and indeed by some amateurs, by polishing or greasing seats to give a bit of

The Cambridge crew of 1911 carrying their boat showing outriggers and sliding seats, both developed some forty years earlier.

backward and forward movement. Even the Greeks of 2,000 years ago had introduced sheepskins onto their wooden seats to allow the oarsmen to slide back and forth a small distance. London Rowing Club took sliding seats to Henley in 1872 and caused a sensation during practice. The seats had an obvious benefit over fixed seats and were introduced to the Boat Race in 1873 when Cambridge won in a record time. At this stage the slide was only about 9 inches. It was not until 1885 that longer runners were introduced, allowing a slide of 15 inches, which is still short by modern standards, where runners are 32½ inches.

As equipment changed, so coaching techniques had to keep pace. In the early days older boys would coach the younger boys and at Shrewsbury, for example, it was not until the late 1860s that the school employed a rowing coach. At the beginning of the twentieth century there existed two definite styles of rowing: the so-called 'orthodox' style and the Fairbairn style. Dodd writes: 'The fountainhead of orthodoxy was the schoolmaster R. S. de Havilland (Havi) who coached the first eight at Eton College from 1893 to 1914, during which time his crews won the Ladies' Plate at Henley 12 times.' The orthodox style had its roots in fixed seat rowing and focused on the body swing. The crews looked uniform and well drilled and Eton's success could not be doubted.  (continues on page 18.)

Steve Fairbairn, acknowledged by most to be the greatest influence on modern rowing technique. Australian by birth, Fairbairn devoted forty years of his life to coaching colleges and clubs in Britain.

Abingdon School fours in 1870 rowing in the orthodox style. H. R. Hayward, a schoolboy rower and later Archdeacon of Cirencester and Residentiary Canon of Gloucester Cathedral, wrote: '[rowing] is so well calculated to turn out men of pluck, men of energy, men of self-denial, men of obedience, and last (but not least) men of perfect sympathy who shall "keep good time" with those with whom they have to work!'

EATING AND TRAINING

The late champion sculler, Renforth, on the Tyne by S. Hull, 1871. James Renforth became the World Sculling Champion in 1868. He developed his strong upper body working as a smith's striker in Gateshead.

Although the study of nutrition and athletes' diets is a relatively modern science, observations on eating, drinking and training have been prevalent since the middle of the nineteenth century. The Victorians, interested as they were in hygiene and physical well-being, were also concerned about what was put on their athletes' plates. There were gaps in what we now recognise as essential knowledge. The importance of hydration, for example, was not properly understood until well after the Second World War. Marathon runners competing in the 1948 Olympic Games were advised not to take on any water on the day before the race and to eat a teaspoon of honey just before they set off to soak up excess liquid. Almost a century earlier the Harvard crews were only allowed three glasses of water a day and had no baths for three weeks leading up to a race, so that often the rowers raced in a severely weakened condition and were covered in boils. In

Oxford, in 1866, Archibald MacLaren published a treatise on physical training, emphasising the importance of diet, sleep, exercise, bathing and fresh air. Commenting on the favoured fad of his day, which was that egg and sherry should be given as a stimulant to men just before they were getting into a boat, he said that the wine would affect the man's nervous system and 'the egg will remain in his stomach as egg until long after the race is over and it will aid him no more than if it had been put in his pocket.'

Rowing training is gruelling for those competing at the top level and it was ever thus. Crews from the Thames Rowing Club preparing for Henley Royal Regatta in the 1870s began in April training in 'heavy boats' which helped to build up muscle and endurance. This was carried out five nights a week on the Tideway between Putney and Barnes. They also did land work, running 2 miles along the towpath three evenings a week plus a hard walk on Sundays. Only in the final month before Henley were they allowed to move into racing boats. When they got to Henley the week before the regatta they would have an outing a day but no rowing on Sundays. So coaches would encourage walking and running. One of the Thames crew, Piggy Eyre, used to walk with his crew from Henley to Boulter's Lock where they would have lunch and then return to Henley, either walking hard or running. It was a full 10 miles on a full stomach and ale.

Today training for the top-level rowers is carefully balanced in order to have crews fit to their maximum in time for major events. A combination of land-training, including

weights and rowing machine or 'erg' (for ergometer) sessions, and water-training is practised by all rowers aiming to race, though the number of sessions and intensity of the training of course reflects the levels of competition from club regattas right up to the Olympic Games. Four-time Olympic gold medal winner, Matthew Pinsent, calculated that he rowed 10,000 kilometres a year while training.

Training on the Isis in the floods of 1872 meant vast areas of water were available to the crews. One bowman complained that when they 'rushed' the hedges in the eight he came away scratched and battered from the experience – not a common rowing injury.

Below: At times rowing was not possible. There were sixteen severe winters in the nineteenth century. This photograph, taken in 1895, shows a coach and six on the ice close to Folly Bridge in Oxford.

However, the introduction of sliding seats called for a different style. Steve Fairbairn, arguably the most influential rowing coach of all time, arrived in Britain in 1881 as an undergraduate at Jesus College, Cambridge. An Australian by birth, he is credited with changing not just technique but also people's attitude to rowing. From 1904 he coached at Jesus where he achieved remarkable success. His method is probably better described as an approach to rowing: 'a state of mind rather than a set of rules.' He taught his crews to think about rowing all the time they were doing it and to read about it at night when they were not. 'If you can't do it easy, you can't do it at all', was one of his catchphrases, emphasising natural movement. He stressed the perfect togetherness of bladework rather than overall appearance. Another of his famous phrases is as apposite today as it was a century ago: 'Mileage makes champions.' Fairbairn summed up the debate over style as '"pretty pretty" versus honest hard work' and wrote in *The Times* in 1931: 'Never sacrifice work to appearance; but of course style is effect, and honest hard work will give true style eventually.'

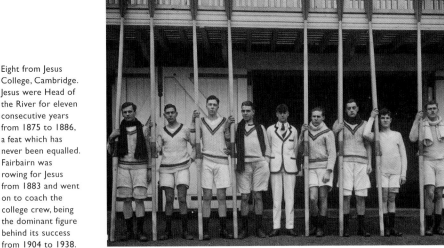

Eight from Jesus College, Cambridge. Jesus were Head of the River for eleven consecutive years from 1875 to 1886, a feat which has never been equalled. Fairbairn was rowing for Jesus from 1883 and went on to coach the college crew, being the dominant figure behind its success from 1904 to 1938.

AMATEUR VERSUS PROFESSIONAL

T HE EARLIEST DEVELOPERS of rowing as a sport for 'gentlemen amateurs' were Eton and Westminster, followed by Oxford and Cambridge. There were no rowing clubs per se on the Thames but small groups of enthusiasts got together to hire out boats and rented rooms above pubs or boatyards as changing rooms. Leander Club, founded originally in Lambeth but based since 1896 in Henley-on-Thames, is recognised to be one of the oldest boat clubs in the world, having been formed in 1818, and it is certainly the most prestigious. Over the course of the century the number of clubs on the major rivers throughout Britain grew and although there was a decline in interest for rowing in the middle years of the century in London, this had more to do with the increase in passenger steamers, which churned up the river, and

A view of the south bank of the Thames, *c.* 1818, where St Thomas's Hospital now stands. Leander rented rack space at Searles' boathouse, on the left, under the shadow of Westminster Bridge.

Leander Club
moved from London
to Henley-on-
Thames in 1897
although it
continued to have
a boathouse in
Putney until the
1960s. Many of the
most famous names
in rowing have been
members of the
Leander Club,
including Steve
Redgrave and
Matthew Pinsent.
By July 2012
members had won
ninety-nine Olympic
medals.

the dreadful pollution; one member of Leander Club lamented in 1857 that 'the river for some miles below Putney is the largest navigable sewer in the world.'

Nevertheless, during the latter half of the nineteenth century, several major clubs were founded on the Thames – London in 1856, Twickenham and City of London Rowing Club in 1860, Molesey in 1866, Vesta in 1870 and Kensington in 1872. The trend was for clubs to be formed upriver, thus getting away from the worst of the traffic and sewerage. Only Curlew at Greenwich, founded in 1866, bucked the trend to move upstream. With the expansion of clubs on the Thames, and on other rivers (Tyne Amateur Rowing Club was formed in 1852, Royal Chester Rowing Club in 1858, and Durham Amateur Rowing Club in 1860), the need to establish a set of rules became a pressing one.

One of the biggest issues to face all sports in the nineteenth century was how to define the difference between the amateur and the professional. 'Amateurism was a crucial aspect of Victorian and Edwardian sport', wrote sports historian Professor Matthew Taylor.

> It was a complex phenomenon that embodied a particular set of principles that opposed making a profit on, or gambling on, sport; an ethos that emphasised sportsmanship and fair play; and an administrative structure based on the creating of voluntary national bodies to regulate sport.

As one of the earliest sports to establish a set of rules, rowing was influential in helping to write the rules for other sports including boxing, football and athletics.

In 1847 the first 'Laws of Boat Racing' had been published but did not deal with eligibility. An updated version appeared in 1872 but dealt only with fouling in races. Since rowing grew out of a tradition of racing for wagers it was always going to be difficult to set rules for who could or could not participate at an amateur level. The question of what constituted an amateur was settled in April 1878 and it was an issue that split the rowing community for half a century. Geoffrey Page, historian of London Rowing Club, explained: 'To a Victorian sportsman amateur and gentleman were synonymous. Tradesmen, artisans, labourers, and watermen were not gentlemen and so, by definition, were not amateurs.' It was not a question of prize money, it was a matter of how a man earned his living. A man would be barred from entering an amateur race if he had 'ever been employed in or about boats or in manual labour' or was a 'mechanic, artisan or labourer'. The following year, in 1879, the Metropolitan Rowing Association was formed and its name changed to the Amateur Rowing Association (ARA) in 1882 and British Rowing in 2009. In 1884 the ARA agreed to the set of rules defining the amateur, adding a clause that nobody could be an amateur who 'was a member of a boat or rowing club containing anyone liable to disqualification under the above rules.'

The Royal Chester Rowing Club is the oldest on the River Dee and has enjoyed royal status since 1840, though its first regatta was held in June 1819 to mark the anniversary of King George III's birthday.

There was an immediate backlash to the ARA's rules on amateurism. Several clubs and a number of distinguished individuals cried foul and in 1890 set up a rival organisation, the National Amateur Rowing Association, which was deliberately socially inclusive. The NARA's leading light, Dr Frederick Furnivall, wrote:

> ... for a university to send its earnest intellectual men into [a city] settlement to live and help working men in their studies and sports, while it sends its rowing men into the ARA to say to these working men, 'You're labourers; your work renders you unfit to associate and row with us', is facing both ways, an inconsistency and contradiction which loyal sons of the university ought to avoid.

Furnivall was passionately opposed to discrimination and in addition to coaching the boat club affiliated to the London Working Men's College where he taught, he founded a club for women at Hammersmith that became known as the Furnivall Sculling Club (see 'Women's Rowing', page 47).

The issue of amateurism had unforeseen consequences, particularly for foreign crews coming to compete at Henley. In 1920 Jack Kelly Senior, the father of Grace, later Princess Grace of Monaco, who won two gold medals that year in the Summer Olympics in the single scull and double sculls, was barred from rowing at Henley because he had worked as a bricklayer in Philadelphia. In 1928 the Olympic champion Bob Pearce, from Australia, was similarly barred because he was a carpenter. Ironically, when he returned to row at Henley in 1931 as a Canadian working as a whiskey salesman he was allowed to enter and won the Diamond Sculls. But the boat that rocked the ARA and the Henley Stewards, forcing a change, was the 1936 Australian national eight. Preparing for the Berlin Olympics, they were excluded from the Grand Challenge Cup at Henley because the crew was composed of policemen who were deemed to be 'manual workers'. This caused embarrassment both for the ARA and the Stewards of Henley Royal Regatta so the following June references to manual labourers, mechanics, artisans and menial duties were deleted from the ARA rules, with Henley following suit.

Dr Frederick Furnivall (1825–1910), who believed in equality and fair chances for everyone who wanted to row.

Jack Kelly Senior, rowing with his son, Jack Kelly Junior, in Philadelphia. Jack Kelly Senior was the first oarsman to become a triple Olympic gold medallist; Jack Kelly Junior represented the United States in four consecutive Olympic Games from 1948.

Reading Ladies' Four 1907: bow – D. Burr; 2 – S. Vigo; 3 – R. Jesse; stroke – J. Haslam.

RACING: PRINCIPLES AND TRADITIONS

RACES FOR ALL ROWING BOATS are organised in categories that pit boat type and experience level against one another and, at junior level, in age groups. The most familiar races are regatta, or side-by-side races, which are held during the late spring and summer months. The standard internationally recognised distance for a regatta is 2,000 metres, with 1,000 metres for adaptive rowing, that is to say for people with a disability, and some junior categories, but many regattas rowed at club level and on rivers are competed for over shorter distances, from 500-metre sprints to 1,250 metres. Here races are rowed in heats and finals. Another type of race is the head race, first introduced in Britain in 1926 by Steve Fairbairn. The head race is a long- distance time-trial between two points on a river and is rowed over a greater distance than a regatta. The most famous head race on the Thames is the Head of the River, rowed annually

The Great Race between Robert Coombes and Charles Campbell for the Championship of the Thames, 1846.

EVESHAMS JUNIOR CREW 1911 WINNERS AT II REGATTAS OUT OF II

Rowing clubs, such as Evesham, have always taken pride in their junior squads.

in March, for eights. This is the Fairbairn head race as he intended it. It is rowed downstream on the Thames from Mortlake to Putney over the same course, but in the opposite direction to the Boat Race. The distance is 4¼ miles. The longest head race in Britain is the Boston Marathon which is rowed in September from Lincoln to Boston, a distance of 31 miles. The fastest time ever recorded for this event is 2 hours and 59.45 minutes but most crews take between four and five hours to complete the course, which involves climbing out of the boat and lifting it, blades and all, over a lock.

The Fours Head on the Tideway is a dramatic spectacle with upwards of four hundred boats competing. It is rowed on the same course as the Boat Race but in the opposite direction and is one of several head races that take place between October and March each year.

A quad from Magdalen College School about an hour into the Boston Marathon in 2007.

A third type of race is the bumps race. These are held in Oxford, where they are known as Torpids and Summer Eights, or Town Bumps for the non-University competition, and in Cambridge, where they are known as Lent Bumps and May Bumps, as well as between London Medical and Veterinary Schools (the United Hospital Bumps), and on the Tideway between old rivals Eton and Shrewsbury. Crews are lined up along the river at regular intervals and all start at the same time. The aim of the race is to catch up with the boat in front and to avoid being caught by the boat behind. A 'bump' is recorded when one crew catches up and overlaps with the one in front. These are fiercely fought races that take place over several days, with the start order changing at the end of each day of racing. The ultimate prize is to be crowned Head of the River. These races provide excellent spectator sport as collisions occur and passions run high.

Although Henley Royal Regatta and the Boat Race are the rowing events best known to the general public, there are many other famous races whose origins date back to the nineteenth century or earlier. These are raced not only

A women's division of May Bumps at Cambridge. May Bumps have been a part of the rowing calendar since the nineteenth century and are enthusiastically followed by coaches, students and the general public who enjoy the colourful spectacle.

on the Thames but on the Dee at Chester, on the Wear at Durham and on the Tyne at Newcastle and there are many other local regattas and head races that take place throughout the year, organised by clubs. In addition to the Head of the River Race there is the amateur championship of the Thames known as the Wingfield Sculls. The race was devised in 1830 by a barrister called Henry Wingfield, who was keen to encourage sculling. He presented the silver challenge sculls and the race has been rowed annually ever since with the exception of the years during the two world wars. The Wingfield Sculls, the Diamond Sculls at Henley and the London Cup at the Metropolitan Regatta make up the 'Triple Crown' of the three premier amateur single sculling events in Britain, though the Wingfield is the oldest. Great names have enjoyed significant wins in this prestigious event, including A. A. Casamajor, who won it six times between 1855 and 1860; Jack Beresford, seven times in succession between 1920 and 1926; and more recently Steve Redgrave, five times between 1985 and 1989. Three-time world champion single sculler Peter Haining from Scotland set a record in 1994 when he became the first man to row the course in under twenty minutes. This record was overturned in 2011 by Adam Freeman-Pask of Imperial College, who knocked 17 seconds off Haining's record with a time of 19 minutes, 41 seconds – only the second time the 20-minute barrier had been broken.

Champion's medal awarded to Charles R. Harding by the proprietors of *The Sportsman* on defeating T. Sullivan for the Championship of England and the Sportsman's Challenge Cup on the Tyne, 16 February 1895.

In 2011 Adam Freeman-Pask of Imperial College Boat Club became only the second man in the history of the Wingfield Sculls to win the race in under twenty minutes.

THE
BOAT RACE

PROGRAMME & PORTRAITS

Published by the National Union of Students
of the Universities and University Colleges
of England and Wales

6ᴰ

G. R. DAY.

THE BOAT RACE

MENTION THE BOAT RACE to anyone and it conjures up a mental image. For some it is the harbinger of spring; for others a titanic battle between the two great universities which marks an annual spectacle on the Thames; for many Oxbridge alumni it is something more visceral. Of course there are detractors, but they are lone voices in the cheering crowds that line the banks of the Thames from Putney to Mortlake, to catch a glimpse of the Dark Blues and the Light Blues chasing the stream on the incoming tide. The Boat Race crops up in literature, in poetry, in film. Over the course of its almost two-hundred-year history it has become an institution and a peculiarly English one at that.

The Oxford and Cambridge Boat Race is a private match between the boat clubs of the two universities. It started as a challenge by Charles Merivale, a student at St John's College, Cambridge, to his school friend from Harrow, Charles Wordsworth, who was studying at Christ Church College, Oxford. Each suggested the idea to their respective captains and on 20 February 1829 a resolution was passed by the University Boat Club at Cambridge that 'Mr Snow, St John's, be requested to write immediately to Mr Staniforth, Christ Church, Oxford, proposing to make up a University Match'. This was not the first of its kind: a university cricket match had been founded by Wordsworth two years earlier. The race was to be rowed 2¼ miles upstream from Hambleden Lock to Henley Bridge.

Rowing had started in both university cities in the late 1700s and the first recorded race for boats with eight oars in Oxford was in 1815 when Brasenose were Head of the River. The races gained in popularity. At Cambridge rowing in eights was slower to take off but they formed their university boat club in 1828, a full decade before the Oxford University Boat Club was established. As on the Isis in Oxford, so on the Cam in Cambridge, races were held in the spring and summer terms between the colleges and the popularity of the sport increased quickly, causing Trinity Hall tutor Leslie Stephen to write about the influence of rowing on undergraduates:

Opposite:
The Centenary
Boat Race official
programme,
23 March 1929.

Oxford University Boat Club Barge, moored alongside Christ Church Meadow in 1871.

The Oxford and Cambridge Rowing Match at Henley on Thames, drawn by W. Havell, engraved by John Pye II and reproduced in Peacock's Polite Repository or Pocket Companion (1829).

It goes on all the year round, and interferes with his studies; it requires a great deal of very hard and disagreeable work; it rubs holes in his skin, raises blisters on his hands, and gives him a chance of an occasional ducking; when pursued to excess, it may even injure his health for life; and it gives him the excuse for periodical outbursts of hilarity, which, if skilfully managed, may lead into scrapes with the authorities.

At first Oxford had no boathouse but in 1846 OUBC paid £180 for a large pleasure barge, 'lately belonging to the Merchant Taylor's Company'. A further £20 was paid for cushions, curtains, awning and extras and a similar amount for men's wages, carriage to London and hire of a horse for bringing the boat back along the towpath to Oxford. The idea of a barge as a floating club, where members could prepare for rowing and relax afterwards, took off: by the end of the nineteenth century all Oxford colleges had a barge, and these were particularly popular during the annual Summer Eights. Cambridge has fewer but larger colleges than Oxford, so that the prestige of the boat clubs is greater. Rather than barges, the clubs took over boat yards on the Cam on the north side of Midsummer Common and built boathouses along the river, with Christ's distinctive blue-and-white house on its own to the left of Victoria Road bridge and the Selwyn, Churchill and King's College boathouse at the other end of the stretch.

College loyalty was replaced by university rivalry for the first Boat Race in Henley. Nothing has changed and passions run equally high in the twenty-first century. The newspapers estimated that 20,000 spectators turned out to watch that first race. Every road was thronged with pedestrians, horsemen, gigs and carriages while the river was crowded with all manner of boats from

Overleaf: Cambridge University Boating Costumes in the nineteenth century.

Summer Eights at Oxford 1922 with Trinity College barge in the centre background and Wadham College barge downstream. Merton College eight is stroked by Sandy Irvine, who two years later disappeared on Mount Everest with George Mallory.

Jesus

Caius College.

Trinity College.

Trinity Hall.

St John's College (Lady Margaret).

Clare College.

Pembroke College.

Emmanuel College.

lege.

Downing College.

Queens' College.

Corpus College.

Magdalene College

St Catharine College.

Christ's College.

King's College.

The Goldie Boathouse, built in 1882, is the oldest surviving intact boathouse on the Cam. It is named after a famous oarsman, John Goldie, who rowed for St John's and the University, competing in four Boat Races against Oxford from 1869 to 1872.

Two pretty symphonies in blue by Ernest Cox, one garbed in dark blue with the Oxford Arms, the other in light blue with the Cambridge Arms.

Two pretty symphonies in blue.

London, Eton and Oxford. The *Jackson's Oxford Journal* reporter was enraptured by the scene:

The splendid scenery, the beautiful river, on which were boats of every description, and the immense company, made a picture of so superb, of so unique a nature that none but those who saw it can form an adequate idea of its richness and variety.

As the Oxford crew rowed down to the start, the spectators could see their black straw hats with broad blue ribbons, jerseys with large horizontal dark blue stripes and their canvas trousers. The Cambridge men wore white with pink neckties. There were no agreed rules so these had to be made up as they went along. Soon after the start the crews clashed and a restart was ordered. The second time, Oxford managed to get clear water ahead of Cambridge and won the race by several lengths. The roar of delight that met Oxford's win echoed round the hills above Henley and fireworks were set off in the town that night to celebrate.

After the first boat race there were several attempts to arrange another match but it was not until 1836 that they succeeded, rowing this time on the Thames in London, from Westminster to Putney. Cambridge was given a light blue Eton ribbon tied on the bows for luck. The crew wore white jerseys while the Oxford crew wore white jerseys with dark blue stripes. In 1839 the universities met for a third time. Cambridge had by now added light blue to their jerseys and thus they became the Light Blues while Oxford were the Dark Blues. Both crews were steered by university men and not professional coxswains, something which became custom, although initially risky, since coxes in those days often had to navigate through the crowds of boats. As the Hon G. Denman from the Cambridge University Boat Club remarked in 1840: 'There were no police arrangements for keeping the course clear and it was often ticklish work for the coxswains to decide whether to go ahead or astern of a train of barges catering across the river.'

The Boat Race came to be fixed on the stretch of river from Putney to Mortlake in 1849 and attracted crowds of thousands with its carnival atmosphere. By the end of the nineteenth century the results of the race were as eagerly awaited by cable in Calcutta, New York and Sydney as any intelligence about a government decision, or the result of a great battle.

The Tideway by Annabel Eyres showing the most important landmarks along the course, which is rowed upstream for the Boat Race and downstream for the Head of the River races.

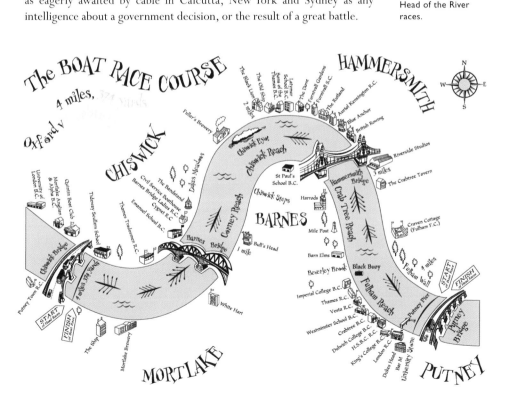

Gold sovereign used to toss for stations for the Oxford and Cambridge Boat Race. The sovereign is kept safely from year to year so that the crews are not corrupted by the idea of rowing for money.

Boris Rankov umpired the Boat Race in 2003, 2005 and 2009. He helped to lead Oxford to victory in the Boat Race six times between 1978 and 1983, three times in the four-seat and three times in the five-seat.

The rules of the Boat Race have changed little. After the 1840 race C. J. Selwyn, a rower and umpire of the Boat Race, set out the principles: 'First, gentlemen should steer; second, that fouling should be abolished; and last, not least, that victory should be its own reward.' There was debate about whether amateur or professional coaches should be used but by the mid-1850s it was resolved in favour of amateur coaches with the exception of the incident when Oxford asked Matthew Taylor in 1857 to instruct them on how to make his keel-less boat go as fast as possible.

In the twenty-first century the rules for the race are essentially the same with a little clarification: the crews must keep to their stations (Middlesex or Surrey) unless they have a lead of clear water; both crews must row through the centre arches of Hammersmith and Barnes bridges. And finally, the Boat Race is always umpired by an 'old blue', with an ex-Cambridge umpire alternating year on year with an ex-Oxford umpire.

Since 1856 the Boat Race has been an annual event. By the mid-1860s it was so popular that steamers threatened to swamp the crews, so that the following year they were made to travel behind the race, thus making it a better spectacle from the bank. Its popularity has scarcely diminished. From the early twentieth century it was broadcast on radio and subsequently on television, though film footage of the Boat Race was captured as early as 1895. As the rules, the course and the universities do not change, the focus of interest is naturally on the detail. Individual crew members are scrutinised: tallest, smallest, oldest, youngest. Timing points are similarly minutely followed, overtaking points, positions of winning or losing crews at certain bridges; events take on

a disproportionate enormity becoming instant legends. Sinkings (the first in 1859), clashes, mutinies, disputes – all are part of the rich history of the race.

The biggest influence on the outcome of the Boat Race is a combination of factors that lead to a winning streak. As Dodd puts it: 'Winning coaches, winning presidents, winning styles produced winning systems, and in the inevitable dialectical nature of an event which is competitive and annual, losers made war and revolution, and evolved other methods to redress their sense of shame.'

The Boat Race has generated more statistics than any other rowing event and many of them are corralled in a history of the Boat Race written by Richard 'Dickie' Burnell for the 150th anniversary. He himself was a statistic, being a member of the fourth generation in his family to compete in the Race. In the more recent past an extraordinary and probably unique familial situation occurred in 2003, when two pairs of brothers rowed, each in opposing boats. David Livingston and Matt Smith rowed for Oxford while Ben Smith and James Livingston rowed for Cambridge. All four boys had been pupils at Hampton School. The outcome of the race was a record too. The winning margin: 1 foot for Oxford.

There has only been one dead heat in the history of the Boat Race, which was in 1877 and it led to recriminations against the finishing judge and much

The victorious Oxford crew of 1923 (the only win enjoyed by Oxford until 1937). This crew, with their initials stitched into their woollen jumpers, contained Gully Nickalls (of the famous rowing family), Sandy Irvine, and P. Mellon, an American who stroked the crew to win by three-quarters of a length.

The Dead Heat,
24 March 1877 by
Charles Robinson,
showing the eights
in close combat at
the finish at
Mortlake, followed
by the umpire.

Three views of an
illuminated rudder
from the 1877 Boat
Race. It is believed
to be the rudder
from the Cambridge
Boat. Illuminated
rudders and oars
have long been given
to winning crews to
commemorate great
rowing
achievements.

indignation and annoyance by the Oxford supporters who believed their crew had won. *Punch* summed up the race succinctly: Oxford Won, Cambridge Too. The four man in the Oxford boat was Willy Grenfell, later Lord Desborough, who at 6 foot 5 inches was an imposing athlete who captained not only the OUBC but the Athletics Club, was Master of Foxhounds at Oxford and an outstanding fencer. He became a leading light in the Olympic movement and Chairman of the British Olympic Association when it was formed in 1905, one in a line of extraordinarily distinguished men who rowed for one of the two universities.

Although linked only by the fact that they have rowed from Putney to Mortlake for one of the two universities, members of Boat Race crews are nevertheless connected by a certain bond. A high proportion of early-nineteenth-century blues went on to be highly distinguished churchmen; two Prime Ministers, a number of politicians and many distinguished barristers emerged from the tidal battle. Coaches whose names resonate throughout the rowing world include Steve Fairbairn, Harcourt Gold, Gilbert Bourne, and in the twentieth century, Dan Topolski; all were blues. So too were Olympic competitors including Guy Nickalls, Dickie Burnell, Matthew Pinsent and cox Acer Nethercott. Television presenter Dan Snow rowed in three boat races from 1999 to 2001 while Hugh Laurie followed in his father's footsteps, competing in the Cambridge Boat in 1980 when Oxford won by just a canvas.

Hugh Laurie training with the Cambridge crew for the 1980 Boat Race. Oxford won by a canvas.

Official Programme

SATURDAY
JULY 5th.

Royal
Henley Peace Regatta
1919

Price 1/-

HERMON TURNER SERIES Rd. No. 100

HENLEY ROYAL REGATTA

IN MARCH 1839 in Henley Town Hall, Captain Edmund Gardiner proposed:

> … [as] lively interest had been manifested at the various boat races which have taken place on the Henley Reach during the last few years, and the great influx of visitors on such occasions, this meeting is of the opinion that the establishing of an annual regatta, under judicious and respectable management, would not only be productive of the most beneficial results to the town of Henley, but from its peculiar attractions would also be a source of amusement and gratification to the neighbourhood, and the public in general.

The town fathers agreed with Gardiner and appointed Stewards to oversee the whole event. The first Henley Regatta took place on the afternoon of Friday 14 June 1839 and was well attended despite appalling weather in the morning of race day. Over 8,000 men and women came from all over the neighbouring counties by horse, on foot, in carriages, and by boat. Ladies 'in much finery' began to take their seats, setting a tradition which continued into the twenty-first century where the dress code for the Stewards' Enclosure still requires ladies to wear a skirt below the knee and where hats are encouraged. The first regatta was deemed such a success that the following year it was expanded to two days. As its popularity grew and its acknowledged place as the foremost regatta in the world, the two days became three in 1886, four in 1906 and finally five days in 1986 with qualifying races held a week before. It is rowed over the first weekend in July and for years marked the end of the social season.

The regatta was renamed the Henley Royal Regatta in 1851 when Prince Albert became the first royal patron. Since his death every reigning monarch has agreed to become the patron of the regatta and royal visitors are not uncommon.

At the time of the first regatta in 1839, Henley was a sleepy market town nestled at the bottom of the ancient Ridgeway, the chalk ridge of the

Opposite: Henley Royal Regatta was suspended during the First World War but in 1919 a Peace Regatta was rowed, with one-off trophies for the winning crews.

The Order of Races for the first Henley Royal Regatta held in 1839. The Grand Challenge Cup is still raced for in the twenty-first century and is an event for elite eights.

Berkshire Downs that extends from Wiltshire to the Goring Gap. The railway did not reach Henley until 1857 but the town lay on a superb stretch of river and at a distance from Oxford and London that meant oarsmen could bring their boats up or downstream to meet in competition.

At the first Henley there were two main races: the Grand Challenge Cup for eights and the Town Challenge Cup for Fours. The races were started downstream from the town by the island and raced up to Henley Bridge. The starter fired a pistol and the umpire followed on horseback, riding along the towpath. One of the first heats for the Grand Challenge Cup was rowed between Wadham College, Oxford, and First Trinity Boat Club, Cambridge, which Trinity won. Dodd recounts: 'They were congratulated by troops of old Cambridge men and Mr Cooper kindly laid out refreshments for them in his garden, while times for the two heats were compared and the voices of salvation met the voices of doom.' Such voices are still heard all along the river bank at the regatta. The final of the Grand took place at 7pm between First Trinity Boat Club, Cambridge, and the Oxford Etonians. The crews raced neck and neck with eager supporters running alongside on the towpath. At the corner before the bridge, which marks the modern finish line, the crews both put on a spurt and First Trinity pulled ahead to gain the bridge and win by half a length.

Going to Henley Regatta, published by J. Ryman, Oxford, c. 1852.

After the race the Trinity crew got dressed and went to the Committee's stand to receive the Grand Challenge Cup and their medals, a tradition which has continued. Other regattas present medals to the winners either in the boats or, in the case of the Olympic Games, on podia on lakeside pontoons. The crew had to sign a receipt promising to return the cup to the Stewards on the next entrance day, 24 May 1840. The Grand Challenge Cup had been won for the first time and has been competed for every year since 1839 without a break, with the exception of the two world wars. When the crew rowed home the following day they put the Cup in its box in the bows of their boat, *Black Prince*, and rowed towards London 'with hearts lighter, though some heads heavier' but amidst great cheering and flag waving from the crowds gathered along the river bank. They stopped off at Eton to admire the chapel and then spent the night at Thames Ditton and the following day arrived at Westminster where the boat was kept in Searle's boathouse below the Cambridge Subscription Rooms.

As the regatta expanded, so the number of races increased and new cups were presented. In 1841 the Stewards' Challenge Cup was introduced for fours; in 1844 the Diamond Challenge Sculls for single sculls came into the regatta. From 1850 the winners of this prestigious race were presented with a 'Pineapple' cup to keep; in 1845 the Silver Goblets was raced for by pairs and the Ladies' Challenge Plate for club and university eights who were not eligible to compete in the Grand. Further races were introduced as rowing

Large numbers of spectators gathered in punts, barges and on the river bank in 1912 to watch the arrival of the Royal Barge carrying King George V and Queen Mary.

James Parish, cox of Leander Club eight in 1837. It was not until 1868 that fours were steered by oarsmen rather than coxes at Henley, and the importance of the cox is conveyed in this portrait of a respected Leander gentleman. A cox has to earn the trust of a crew and in return he or she can encourage and motivate them even when they are exhausted.

developed and by 2012 the number of events at Henley Royal Regatta totalled twenty, the most recent addition being a race for Junior Women's quadruple sculls in that same year.

By then Henley Royal Regatta had been in existence for 173 years and during that time there have been many memorable experiences that have changed the lives of participants, of the spectators and the nature of the regatta itself. One of the most dramatic, not to say theatrical, challenges to the established order came about in 1868. It all began at the first international rowing regatta in Paris in 1867 where crews from the continent raced against crews from America and Britain. One of the great characters, innovators and outstanding oarsmen of the era was W. B. 'Guts' Woodgate of London Rowing Club. In Paris he saw a four from the Western Club of St John, New Brunswick, rowing without a cox. He learned that the bowman was steering using a lever moved by his foot to manipulate the rudder. The Americans beat crews from France, Germany, Belgium and England and won two finals. Woodgate was impressed. There was controversy over the use of coxes at the time, as there were no rules governing them and colleges were resentful that schools and clubs could use very small boys, which was an advantage. Woodgate announced that in the Stewards' Cup of 1868 he would race without a cox, steering with a foot-guided wire from his seat (three). Their opponents from University College, Oxford, protested, citing custom, since there were no explicit rules. Stewards supported the appeal so Woodgate wrote to the chairman saying he would comply with the conditions at the start of the race but that the cox, Fred Weatherly, would jump overboard once the race had begun. Geoffrey Page, in *Hear the Boat Sing*, describes the event: 'Accordingly, Brasenose went to the start of the Stewards' with a cox, who jumped overboard immediately the race started, to the immense delight of the large crowd that had assembled to see the fun, and to the extreme danger of the cox, who was rescued only with difficulty.' Woodgate's Brasenose crew went on to win the race by 100 yards but was disqualified. The Stewards bowed to the inevitable, however, and the next year a race for coxless fours was introduced. Weatherly, who had a lucky escape from being dragged under by water lilies while fighting his way towards the bank, went on to become a highly successful barrister and song-writer, composing among three thousand other songs the words to 'Danny Boy'.

From the very beginning a popular way to enjoy the racing and other delights of Henley was from the river. College barges, punts, rowing boats and other river craft all jostled for position along the length of the course, sometimes with disastrous results. In 1887 a large royal party visited Henley to mark Queen Victoria's Golden Jubilee. Such was the crush of boats around the barge that the course was effectively narrowed to allow only one boat to pass through. A luckless sculler, Guy Nickalls, found himself embroiled in an undignified crash with the Royal Barge in the final of the Diamond Sculls, which meant that not only did he lose the race to J. C. Gardner of Emmanuel College, Cambridge, but he also broke his boat and blades. Christopher Dodd continues the story:

> However, Guy Nickalls was not put off winning Henley cups by his royal gaffe. In the years between 1887 and 1897 he won the Diamonds five times and the Goblets six times, three of them with his brother Vivian, who also won the Diamonds once. Both brothers were also in winning eights and fours.

The Nickalls family were by any account an impressive clan. Guy's mother, Emily, had become the first woman to climb Mont Blanc and Monte Rosa in one week in the summer of 1868 when she was pregnant. The family spanned three generations at Henley with Guy's son, Gully, rowing successfully in the 1920s, winning the Silver Goblets and Nickalls' Challenge Cup in 1920 and winning silver in the men's eight at the summer Olympics of that year and a further silver in the Amsterdam Olympics in 1928. (Guy had won gold in the 1908 Olympics, also in the eight.) Gully Nickalls became the first sportsman to make an outside broadcast for the BBC in 1927 when covering the Boat Race.

'Look Ahead, Sir!' A Reminiscence of Henley Regatta from The Graphic, July 1880. Before horizontal wooden booms were laid alongside the regatta course at the beginning of the twentieth century, the problem of spectators invading the racing line was significant and one sent up by the cartoonists of the era.

The Club Nautique de Gand in Belgium became the first foreign crew to win the Grand Challenge Cup. They first rowed at the regatta in 1901 and took the coveted prize three times in 1906, 1907 and 1909.

The status of Henley as one of the premier rowing regattas in the world was well established by the end of the nineteenth century and inevitably foreign crews wished to come to race on the most famous stretch of water in England. Although foreigners competed from the 1880s onwards, the first to cause serious ripples on the Thames were the Belgians, who arrived in 1901. The Club Nautique de Gand of Belgium lost to Leander in the final of the Grand but became the first foreign crew to win the cup in 1906. Foreign crews were regarded by some with hostility but by others with interest and some bemusement. In 1901 the University of Pennsylvania sent a crew from Philadelphia. They were viewed as something of a novelty both for their rowing style, which was a short stroke and without body swing, but also for their teetotal training regime and lack of liberty so that the crew were 'kept to their quarters almost as strictly as prisoners'. Another aspect that interested a journalist from the *Field* was that their coach, Ellis Ward, 'performs his duties in America from a launch and cannot ride either a horse or a bicycle' – this proved difficult at Henley as regatta rules forbade launches on the course. In the end an Englishman took pity on Ward and got permission for him to use the SS *Hibernia* and the crew did all their training downstream of the island.

Women at Henley Royal Regatta have traditionally occupied the river bank, the college barges and provided a decorative presence in the Stewards' Enclosure. It was not until 1993 that the Stewards introduced the Open Women's single sculls, and not until 2000 that the open women's eights were raced in the Remenham Cup, under the same rules as the Grand Challenge Cup. Three years later the Princess Grace Challenge Cup was introduced for quadruple sculls and in 2012 a new race was included for junior women's quadruple sculls.

WOMEN'S ROWING

D R FREDERICK FURNIVALL was one of the energetic spirits behind women's rowing in the nineteenth century. As we have already seen, he set up the Furnivall Sculling Club in 1896. The captaincy of the club was restricted to women until after the Second World War in honour of Furnivall's original idea. Women's rowing was not taken seriously until the late twentieth century but it does not mean there were not female rowers and scullers in earlier times. The oldest rowing club in Britain to accept women was Falcon Rowing Club in Oxford, which was founded in 1869. As early as 1871 a reporter on the *Huddersfield Chronicle and West Yorkshire Advertiser* mused as to when women would be competing for 'the ribbon upon the Thames', given that they raced at regattas in America.

Despite the best efforts of Dr Furnivall and other enthusiasts for women scullers and rowers, the reality is that it took a shockingly long time for women to be accepted at the highest level. As Steve Redgrave wrote in his 2011 book, *Great Olympic Moments*:

Amy Gentry in a single scull, 1932. Amy was British single sculls rowing champion for three years running in the 1930s and retired undefeated. After the First World War she helped to form a women's section of Weybridge Rowing Club, founding the Weybridge Ladies' Amateur Rowing Club in 1926.

In my own sport, rowing, women were not allowed to compete in the Olympics until 1976, and even then they were limited to a distance of 1,000 metres. For most of the [twentieth] century women were barred from almost all endurance sports, because it was feared that the delicacy of their condition (i.e. being female) would cause them to collapse or, worse, appear unladylike.

Nevertheless there are records showing that from around 1830 women began to form racing crews in British rowing clubs though from the 1880s until the 1920s the majority of women's competitive rowing events were 'style events', that is to say that the crews were judged on the most elegant style.

The Women's Amateur Rowing Association was formed in 1923 and four years later all-women crews from Oxford and Cambridge Universities raced at Henley-on-Thames in the first of what became the annual Henley Boat Races. The development of women's rowing was painfully slow, despite this early surge after the First World War, which also saw the first Women's Eights Head of the River Race. By 1960 it was estimated that there were still fewer than a thousand women rowers in Britain. Even when women's rowing was finally introduced into the Olympic Games in 1976 there was a sense that the

Henley Women's Regatta has colour and atmosphere and has become a favourite with foreign crews as well as the British clubs.

serious competition was between the men. It was a frustrating time to be a female oarswoman. However, rowing carried on and developed; the Women's Boat Race became a fiercely fought annual event at Henley and more women's races were introduced into the national regatta programme.

Eventually in 1987 Britain's women's national coach, Rosie Mayglothling, who had won the invitation double sculls at Henley Royal Regatta in 1982 when the Stewards had briefly introduced women's events as an experiment, proposed a women's regatta at Henley to be rowed shortly before the Henley Royal. She canvassed opinion and found a receptive audience, though all acknowledged there were serious hurdles to be overcome, not least convincing the Stewards of Henley Royal Regatta that this was something they could support. After much careful, quiet diplomacy and a few teething problems in the early years, Henley Women's Regatta grew and developed. It is now an annual fixture, rowed over three days in the middle of June from Temple Island to Remenham Farm, where the crowds, friends, supporters and rowing enthusiasts gather in their thousands, their cheers echoing off the hills every bit as loudly as they did when the first Henley regatta was held in 1839. By 2012, when it celebrated its twenty-fifth anniversary, Henley Women's Regatta offered nearly thirty events for over three hundred crews.

A few strokes into a race at Henley Women's Regatta the crews pass the beautiful temple on The Island.

THE OLYMPIC GAMES

Rowing was one of the founding sports of the modern Olympic Games, although the water at Piraeus was too rough for rowing in 1896 so it was not until 1900 in Paris that British crews took part in their first Olympic regatta. A total of 108 rowers from eight nations competed and France won six medals out of four events: single sculls, coxed pairs, coxed fours and eights. Britain took just one medal, a bronze, in the single sculls and came bottom of the medal table. The 1908 Games were hosted by London and the rowing events were held at Henley. Here the home team dominated, winning gold in all four disciplines and silver in three. The inter-war Olympic Games saw some great rivalries and friendships established. The American Jack Kelly Senior, who had been excluded from Henley in 1920, won the single sculls ahead of one of Britain's most successful rowers of all time, Jack Beresford. The Briton became the first man in the history of Olympic sport to win five medals at five consecutive Games. That is, until his outstanding record was beaten in 2000 when another Briton, Steve Redgrave, won a fifth gold medal in five consecutive Olympic regattas, eclipsing Beresford, whose tally was three golds and two silvers.

The 1948 Olympic Games were the first to be held after the Second World War and became known as the Austerity Games, principally for the fact that they were run on a shoestring budget by the British. The rowing at Henley was enthusiastically attended by huge crowds, despite steady rain and cold conditions, and they were not disappointed. Jack Wilson and Ran Laurie, father of oarsman and actor Hugh Laurie, won gold for Great Britain in the coxless pairs. Both Wilson and Laurie had been out in the Sudan and not rowed in nearly a decade since they won the Silver Goblets at Henley in 1938 but they came together to win the Goblets once again and then their Olympic title. In the double sculls, Dickie Burnell and Bert Bushnell beat a strong Danish crew by two lengths and Charles Burnell, who had

Opposite:
Jack Beresford was the most successful oarsman of his generation and the only man in history to win the Wingfield Sculls, Championship of the Thames, in seven consecutive years.

Jack Beresford and Dick Southwold at the 1936 Berlin Olympics. They won gold in the double sculls taking Beresford's total to five medals in five consecutive Olympic Games, a record not beaten until 2000 when Steve Redgrave won his fifth gold in Sydney.

This rowing vest was worn by Bobby Collins in the coxed four at Henley-on-Thames in the Olympic regatta in 1948. He said, 'When we were issued with white sleeveless singlets, we felt very naked.'

won gold in the eight in 1908, watched his son making history as they became the first father and son to win gold medals at two Olympic Games. Even if the record is ever matched it is most unlikely that the events will have both been won at the same venue. The eight were successful in their final, winning silver. As a result, Great Britain topped the rowing medals table but this was a high-water mark in their showing for sixty years.

The year 1952 marked a sea change in the rowing regattas at the Olympic Games, as the Eastern Bloc countries began to weigh in with immensely strong crews but with accusations of doping and other irregularities placed at their doors over the next decades. In 1964 Britain won a silver medal in the coxless fours, but it was the United States of America, Russia and Germany who dominated the Olympic rowing tables in those years. Then, in 1968 a new country came to the fore: East Germany. At their first Olympic Games they topped the medal table and in 1972 only New Zealand winning gold in the eights was able to break the hold on the regatta by the East Germans and the Soviet Union. In 1976 women's events were introduced and all the gold medals were won by women from East Germany or Bulgaria.

The 1984 Games were held in Barcelona and this was the start of the Redgrave era with his first gold in the coxed four with Richard Budgett, Martin Cross, Andy Holmes and cox Adrian Ellison. In 1991 Jürgen Grobler became coach of the men's Olympic squad and has achieved almost legendary status, with gold medals at every Olympic Games from 1972 (with East Germany) to 2008. In Sydney in 2000, as Steve Redgrave was making history by winning his fifth Olympic Gold medal in consecutive games and the men's eight pulled off a spectacular victory also to win gold, Britain's women took

Steve Redgrave training with Andy Holmes, with whom he won a gold medal in the coxless pairs in Seoul in 1988. They had previously won gold in the 1984 Olympic regatta in Los Angeles in a coxed four with Richard Budgett, Martin Cross and cox Adrian Ellison.

their first Olympic medal, a silver in the women's quadruple sculls, a crew that included Katherine Grainger, one of the undisputed outstanding women scullers of her generation with three Olympic silver medals and six World Championship gold medals to her name by the end of 2011. In 2008 in Beijing Britain were on top of the rowing medals table for the first time since 1948 with two golds (one for Zac Purchase and Mark Hunter in the lightweight double sculls and the other for the coxless four), two silvers (for the men's eight and the women's quadruple sculls), and a bronze for the women's pair, Elise Laverick and Anna Bebbington. This was the year that Adaptive Rowing was first introduced to the Paralympic Games and British scullers Tom Aggar and Helene Raynsford won gold medals in the single sculls disciplines, while the mixed coxed four won bronze.

In 2012 the Olympic Games regatta was rowed at Dorney Lake, home of Eton College rowing, completing the circle that began nearly two hundred years earlier when Eton and Westminster codified the rules of amateur rowing.

Steve Redgrave at Sydney, August 2000, after winning his fifth Olympic Gold Medal with crew members Tim Foster, James Cracknell and Matthew Pinsent. Redgrave and Pinsent won gold in Barcelona in the coxless pairs in 1992 and in the same event in Atlanta in 1996.

Katherine Grainger, at stroke, one of the most successful oarswomen of all time, celebrating a win in the double sculls with Anna Watkins on Lake Karapiro in New Zealand at the 2010 World Rowing Championships.

FURTHER READING

Burnell, Richard. *One Hundred and Fifty Years of the Oxford and Cambridge Boat Race*. Precision Press/Guinness, 1980.

Burnell, Richard and Page, Geoffrey. *Brilliants: History of the Leander Club*. Leander Club, 1997.

Dodd, Christopher. *The Oxford & Cambridge Boat Race*. Stanley Paul, 1983.

Dodd, Christopher. *Henley Royal Regatta*. Stanley Paul, 1987.

Dodd, Christopher. *The Story of World Rowing*. Stanley Paul, 1992.

Hampton, Janie. *The Austerity Olympics*. Aurum, 2008.

Hampton, Janie. *London Olympics 1908 and 1948*. Shire Library, 2011.

Livingston, David and James. *Blood Over Water*. Bloomsbury Publishing, 2010.

Page, Geoffrey. *Hear the Boat Sing. The History of Thames Rowing Club and Tideway Rowing*. Kingswood Press, 1991.

Pinsent, Matthew. *A Lifetime in a Race*. Ebury Press, 2005.

Redgrave, Steve. *A Golden Age – the Autobiography*. BBC Books, 2004.

Sherriff, Clare. *The Oxford College Barges*. Unicorn Press, 2003.

Sherwood, W. E. *Oxford Rowing*. Henry Frowde, 1900.

Matthew Pinsent and Steven Redgrave: Caption to follow.

WEBSITES

www.britishrowing.org is rowing's national governing body. Full of useful links to events and good information about beginning rowing or sculling.

www.worldrowing.com is the official website for international rowing.
Good for information about rowing events worldwide and the Olympic
regattas.

www.rrm.co.uk is the website of the River and Rowing Museum at
Henley. It provides useful information about the history of rowing and
is an excellent museum experience.

www.hrr.co.uk contains all the information you need about visiting
Henley Royal Regatta and has good archive data.

www.hwr.org.uk is the official website for Henley Women's Regatta with
plenty of information and history.

www.theboatrace.org is a treasure trove of facts, details, images and
current news on the Boat Race.

www.furnivall.org has the best gallery of photographs from the history of
women's rowing and friendly web-support for anyone wanting to know
more.

PLACES TO VISIT

The River and Rowing Museum, Mill Meadows, Henley on Thames, Oxon
RG9 1BF. Telephone: 01491 415600. Website: www.rrm.co.uk. This
museum offers an excellent visitor experience for all the family. Superb
galleries, river view, café and shop plus parking.

Henley Royal Regatta takes place during the last week in June annually in
Henley-on-Thames. Open and free of charge to anyone who is happy to
watch one of the greatest annual spectacles from the river bank.
Information on eligibility for ticketed enclosures available from the
website, www.hrr.co.uk.

The Boat Race can be enjoyed either from the river banks on either side of
the London Thames from Putney to Mortlake, in any of the pubs along
the river or, for those who prefer to keep warm and dry, it is an
excellent television spectacle.

Henley Women's Regatta takes place in mid-June in Henley-on-Thames and
welcomes visitors to watch the exciting racing and see the cream of
women's rowing as well as enjoying the party atmosphere, eating, stalls
and good humour.

There are regattas, head races and other rowing events on all major rivers
during the year. Visitors are always welcome to watch events and the
majority are free of charge, or charge for parking or access to the
'enclosure'. Information on events in your area can be found on
www.biddulph.org.uk.

INDEX